Original title:
A Drop of Paradise

Copyright © 2025 Creative Arts Management OÜ
All rights reserved.

Author: Zachary Prescott
ISBN HARDBACK: 978-1-80581-663-8
ISBN PAPERBACK: 978-1-80581-190-9
ISBN EBOOK: 978-1-80581-663-8

## Song of the Springs

A brook sings tunes so sweet,
With frogs doing their dance on repeat.
The fish have all the fun,
While I wish I had a bun.

Splashing water, oh what a jest,
Ducklings quack, they're the best!
They think they own the pond,
While I wave from the frond.

## Essence of Tranquility

Sunshine pours from the sky,
Bees buzzing, oh my, oh my!
Sipping tea on a lawn chair,
Waiting for butterflies to share.

A squirrel scurries, steals my snack,
Chasing him seems quite the knack.
Laughter bubbles like a stream,
Nature's giggles, like a dream.

## The Well of Ecstasy

Giggling flowers share their glee,
Dancing ants, quite the spree!
But watch your step, don't take a dive,
You might just find more than five.

Butterflies waltz on a sunny spree,
Hummingbirds get envious of me!
They sip nectar with such flair,
While I'm left to comb my hair.

## **Veil of Serenity**

Clouds drift by with a hint of sass,
While I'm wondering where the time has passed.
The grass tickles toes, oh what a delight,
As snoozing cats dream of endless night.

Rain drops tap like a friendly tune,
Turtles bicker over who gets the moon.
With nature's laugh echoing wide,
I join the fun, can't let it slide.

## **Elixir of Serenity**

In a cup of dreams, I take a sip,
Giggling softly as my thoughts do flip.
There's a frog in a hat doing a jig,
While I ponder life's secrets, oh so big.

A snail on a dance floor, what a sight!
Busting moves with all its might.
With every chuckle, joy finds its way,
In this bizarre brew, I want to stay.

## **Tides of Celestial Grace**

The waves whisper jokes from the moonlit shore,
While jellyfish giggle and sea turtles snore.
A star fell down, took a tumble and spun,
Said, 'Why so serious? Let's have some fun!'

Crabs in tuxedos, getting ready to dance,
Hey, look at that fish! It's flaunting a prance.
As the tide rolls in, laughter swells high,
In this cosmic circus, we barely ask why.

## Essence of the Divine

In a garden where daisies wear hats made of cheese,
Butterflies chuckle, enjoying the breeze.
A gnome tells a tale that makes daisies blush,
While a rabbit joins in, creating a rush!

Pixies on roller skates zooming around,
Each twist a giggle; joy knows no bound.
A cloud passing by sprinkles laughter anew,
Sprouting smiles in colors, a whimsical hue.

**Raindrops on Blossom**

Raindrops tap-dance on leaves with delight,
While flowers wear smiles, oh what a sight!
A bumblebee buzzes a tune in the air,
Singing to daisies with nary a care.

Puddles form mirrors for clouds to admire,
Each reflection roars laughter, fueling the fire.
As the rain plays games, the sun peeks its head,
In this playful ballet, we'll hop out of bed!

## **Bottled Reverie**

In a jar, I store my glee,
A cork that sings, just wait and see.
With every sip, I giggle wide,
I'm the king of joy, no need to hide.

My potion's made with winks and cheer,
And tickles sprinkled far and near.
One swig, I dance upon the floor,
Another sip? I'm out the door!

When friends arrive, I share my find,
The bubbling laughter, oh so kind.
In Bottled Reverie, we all unwind,
With chortles bubbling, never maligned.

So toast to jars of silly stuff,
The world is wild, but we have enough.
In feathery laughter, we'll forever stay,
For joy's a bottle, come what may.

## A Soothing Bath

The tub awaits with bubbles bright,
As rubber ducks take off in flight.
With sudsy swords, we fight the grime,
In this foamy world, we've got the time.

I bring my book of silly rhymes,
And giggle at my sudsy crimes.
The rubber duck quacks, it steals the show,
While I ponder if it'd like to flow.

A splash here, a splash there, all around,
In my soothing bath, all worries drown.
With corkscrew curls and shampoo dreams,
I float away on bubbly beams.

So soak away the day's long stress,
With laughter's scent, I must confess.
In my soak, life feels so bright,
Just me, the ducks, and pure delight!

## Cascade of Dreams

In the morning light, I take a leap,
With visions dancing, not a peep.
Dreams tumble down like a water slide,
With laughter ringing, I enjoy the ride.

A splash of silly, a twist of fate,
Laughter flows, oh it's never late.
As dreams cascade like a perfect stream,
I giggle and float, lost in the dream.

The clouds are pillows, soft and white,
Kicking back in this dreamy sight.
I'll catch the rainbows on my way,
In this cascade, I'm here to play!

So come, my friends, let's join the fall,
In whimsical waters, we'll have a ball.
For in the joy of our shared day,
The cascade of dreams will lead our way.

## The Glow of Nature

In the garden bright, I find my flair,
With dancing flowers that tease the air.
The sunbeam giggles, tickling my toes,
While the grass whispers secrets that only it knows.

Butterflies flutter in a crazy dance,
Join me, dear bees, let's take a chance!
With each buzzing hum and fluttering wing,
The glow of nature makes my heart sing.

The trees tell tales in rustling tones,
Of squirrels that frolic and little gnomes.
A comedy show in twinkling light,
The glow brings laughter, soft and bright.

So let's stroll through this vibrant hue,
With smiles aplenty and jokes anew.
In The Glow of Nature, all is clear—
Life's a merry jest, let's spread the cheer!

## **Petals in the Rain**

Tiny blooms dance, oh what a sight,
Splashes of color, pure delight!
Umbrellas tip over, folks may frown,
But flowers are laughing, they won't drown!

Puddles are mirrors, giggles abound,
Splashing around, joy is found.
The garden's a stage, nature's grand play,
Who knew wet petals could brighten the day?

## Harmony's Refreshment

Breezy tunes float on a wave,
Bees are buzzing, they misbehave!
Sips of nectar, sweet to taste,
Nature's barista, no time to waste!

Birds on branches sing silly songs,
Worms wear hats, that's where it belongs!
Butterflies mingle, their colors collide,
In this zany place, let's take a ride!

**Sweet Surrender**

Sugary drops fall from the sky,
Candy clouds drift, oh my oh my!
Lemonade rivers, swirl like a dream,
We sip and we laugh, laughter a stream!

Ice cream mountains, we scoop and dive,
In this gooey world, we feel alive!
Chocolate puddles, sticky and bright,
We'll eat our way through day and night!

## **Shimmering Reflection**

Mirrors of fun in a sunlit ray,
Jellyfish wiggling, they sway and play!
Jumping into laughter, the waves all cheer,
What a grand spectacle, joy is near!

Shiny reflections, what do we see?
Funny faces of you and me!
Splash and giggle, let's take a bow,
The ocean's a stage, come join us now!

## Journey to Enchantment

In a field of daisies, I danced with glee,
A squirrel stole my sandwich, laughing with me.
The sun wore shades, sipping lemonade,
While butterflies fluttered, a parade they made.

A rabbit in sneakers raced past with a cheer,
Chasing a dream that was perfectly clear.
With every step, I tripped on a root,
Yet giggled through mud, oh how I looked cute!

A cloud on a whim tried to steal my hat,
I wrestled it down—oh, what of that spat!
We took selfies together, what a fine sight,
As peacocks applauded, their feathers so bright.

At dusk, I looked back on the day full of fun,
My head full of laughter, my heart with the sun.
In this silly escape, nothing felt wrong,
Every moment a lyric, a whimsical song.

## The Allure of Freshness

In the market I spotted a curious pear,
It winked at me slyly, a sweet little dare.
A tomato in red danced, looking so cute,
Juggling some peas while wearing a boot!

The lettuce was gossiping, leafy and spry,
Saying, 'You should try the dip, give it a fly!'
With cilantro so zesty, a twist on the tongue,
Our salad's a party where all are so young.

A cucumber grinned, with a cool, smug face,
While onions just wept, in their layered embrace.
With each bite I took, giggles echoed around,
Freshness exploding, oh joy knows no bound!

As dinner drew near, laughter filled the air,
The veggies united in culinary flair.
We feasted on freshness, and oh what a scene,
The flavor of joy in this garden cuisine!

# Reflection of the Soul

A mirror showed me a cheeky old chap,
With wild hair and a spontaneous clap.
I chuckled at wrinkles that danced on my face,
Embracing imperfections with humorous grace.

In this quirky glass, I found such delight,
A spirit that twirled from morning till night.
Wearing socks with sandals as bold as can be,
Who knew that the mirror could make me so free?

The reflection replied with a wink and a grin,
'Life's a grand circus, so jump right in!'
With each silly pose, the laughter took flight,
A lighthearted dance in the soft evening light.

So here's to the moments we cherish and share,
Embracing the laughter, the love, and the flair.
Reflecting on joy with a heart full of jest,
In the canvas of life, we're surely the best!

## **Breath of the Divine**

A cloud sneezes, rain drops fall,
Puddles form, oh what a sprawl.
Dancing ducks in matching boots,
Waddle round in silly hoots.

Sunshine peeks through misty gray,
Rainbow cows start their ballet.
Jelly beans float in the lake,
Taste them quick, oh for goodness' sake!

Wind whispers jokes, trees start to laugh,
Squirrels join in, adding a gaffe.
Nature's party's quite the scene,
With giggles echoing evergreen.

So let's splash and join the fun,
Beneath the sky, we'll all be one.
With laughter shared among the trees,
We'll soak in joy, just like a breeze.

## The Charm of Stillness

A cat perched high on the fence,
Staring down with defiance intense.
Fish in the pond throw a wink,
As frogs gather near to rethink.

The grasshoppers hold a debate,
Arguing which path is first-rate.
While butterflies wear their best ties,
In secret talks beneath the skies.

Breezes tickle each sleepy leaf,
As nature chuckles in disbelief,
A snail slides by with great intent,
It's late for his important event!

And as the air sits calm and bright,
Birds share gossip, take to flight.
In quiet charm, the world spins round,
In the silliness of silence found.

## Dreamlike Streams

A brook babbles, spilling tales,
Of dragonflies riding on scales.
Turtles in hats swim with flair,
While frogs burst into song with care.

Candy fish swim near the shore,
Balloons tugging at their core.
Unexpected jokes, splashes of fun,
A peachy moon has just begun.

Sunlight flickers, setting the mood,
Trees gossip and tease, oh so shrewd.
Worms in bowties crawl on top,
Their graceful entrance, a big flop!

In this whimsical waterway,
Laughter bubbles, come what may.
As dreamers join in this delight,
The night's warm glow feels just right.

## Dance of the Raindrops

Raindrops tango on the ground,
With splashes making quite the sound.
Giggling gusts join in the show,
As umbrellas bloom in a row.

The puddles burst into a cheer,
Boating rubber ducks near and dear.
Socks get soggy; shoes come off,
Everyone joins in with a scoff.

With every patter, rhythm flows,
Nature's orchestra softly grows.
Little feet stomp with delight,
As rain and laughter unite bright.

So prance with me in muddy shoes,
In this rain dance, there's nothing to lose.
For when the drops come out to play,
We find joy in the wet bouquet.

## Serenity in a Single Seed

In the garden, there's a seed,
Telling tales of life indeed.
Dancing ants in suits of black,
Stealing snacks, then getting back.

Sunshine laughs with rays so bright,
While clouds giggle in pure delight.
A flower yawns, stretches awake,
Wonders if it's time for cake.

Bees in bow ties hum a tune,
Flirting with a passing moon.
A worm in shades, so very cool,
Wiggles in a garden pool.

Blowing kisses to the breeze,
Nature's laughter, if you please.
Life is silly, light and sweet,
In this patch of green retreat.

# Whispers of Eden

In the orchard, squirrels play,
Chasing dreams, or nuts, hooray!
Birds wearing hats sing a rhyme,
Complaining 'bout the lack of time.

Grapes in clusters gossip low,
"Is it me, or is it slow?"
Pigs in shades sip lemonade,
Planning their next grand parade.

A breeze arrives, does a jig,
Tickling leaves, it's such a gig!
In this Eden, giggles spill,
Every moment, joy's the thrill.

While butterflies wear polka dots,
Adding flair to all the plots.
Nature's stage, with laughs galore,
Whispers echo forever more.

## The Liquid Jewel

In a pond, a splash and cheer,
Frogs declare, "We rule right here!"
A shiny drop rolls off a leaf,
Turns to laughter, turns to grief.

Fish in suits swim by in style,
Telling jokes, they wink and smile.
A dragonfly juggles flies,
While all the water lilies rise.

Crickets chirp a serenade,
Underneath the shimmering shade.
As evening falls, they raise a glass,
To all the fun that comes to pass.

Raindrops laugh and tease the sky,
While puddles giggle, oh my, oh my!
In this realm of watery joy,
Nature's antics we enjoy!

## **Serene Cascade**

Down the hill, waters flow,
Carrying laughter, soft and low.
Pebbles dance, from side to side,
Chasing ripples, their funny ride.

A duck in boots quacks a tune,
Head bobbing to the afternoon.
Turtles join with slowest speed,
Swimming past, they take the lead.

Bubbles rise like giggling friends,
Spreading joy that never ends.
In the splashes, secrets hide,
Nature's jesters, full of pride.

As sunset wraps the day in gold,
The cascade shares its stories told.
With laughter echoing so clear,
In the calm, we find our cheer.

## The Whispering Stream

In the forest deep and wide,
The stream spills secrets, bonafide.
It giggles past the rocks and trees,
Whispering jokes with the buzzing bees.

With every splash, it starts to tease,
Silly fish dance like they're at ease.
They wear their smiles like a badge,
While frogs croak tunes, what a badge!

Oh, the current winks and sighs,
While passing ducks make funny cries.
They quack about the silliest things,
Like who can wear the best of blings.

So if you stroll where waters glee,
Listen close, you might just see,
A joyful splash, a playful dream,
In the midst of nature's funny scheme.

## Oasis of Light

In a desert vast, where sun's ablaze,
An oasis jests, in mirage plays.
Palm trees sway with a cheeky grin,
Inviting folks to jump right in.

The sand's so hot, it starts to dance,
As water sparkles, it takes a chance.
A camel struts in sunglasses cool,
Looks like he's breezing back from school.

Lizards spin tales of the heat,
While cactus wear hats, looking neat.
The clouds above play hide and seek,
As smiles bloom in this sunny sneak.

So when you find this bright delight,
Join the laughter, bask in light.
In the khaki kingdom, join the spree,
And laugh along as wild and free.

## Imprints of Joy

On a beach where footprints sway,
Little waves giggle and play.
They chase the gulls with little peeps,
Telling stories of hidden heaps.

A crab with swagger, steps so bold,
Sports a shell as bright as gold.
He pinches fun, just to tease,
While kids giggle, racing the breeze.

Seagulls squawk, 'Oh what a sight!'
As sunbeams dance with pure delight.
The sandcastles, tall and proud,
Wave a hello to every crowd.

So leave your cares upon the shore,
Join the laughter, come and explore.
In this playground where joy unfolds,
Every grain has a story told.

## Tales of the Cascade

In the mountain's heart, a waterfall sings,
Gushing forth with giddy flings.
It splashes rocks in a cheeky game,
While toads lip-sync, bringing fame.

Mossy stones chuckle in delight,
As rainbow spray catches the light.
"You can't catch me!" the water shouts,
While curious squirrels skitter about.

The trees join in with rustling laughs,
As critters sketch their quirky paths.
Life's a dance on water's edge,
With every trickster making a pledge.

So if you wander where laughter flows,
Hear the cascades and how it goes.
In every droplet, a jolly spin,
Join the fun, let the tales begin.

## **Whispers of Eden**

In a garden where the gnomes laugh,
They tiptoe through the sunlit path.
With flowers wearing polka dots,
And bumblebees that dance in spots.

The apples giggle, ripe and round,
Squirrels gossip from the ground.
A rabbit with a bowtie grin,
Plays hopscotch with a spinning pin.

The clouds above make silly shapes,
Like cats and hats and fishy drapes.
While butterflies with crowns of lace,
Float by in a comical race.

Oh, in this space where dreams unfold,
The tales of whimsy never grow old.
With every laugh and joyful cheer,
This joyful place, we hold so dear.

## **Nectar on the Breeze**

Buzzing bees with jokes to share,
Steal sweet nectar from the air.
While hummingbirds with twisty rolls,
Play tag around the flowers' poles.

The fountain gurgles, sings a tune,
While squirrels juggle nuts by noon.
Lemonade falls from the trees,
And sunshine drips like sticky bees.

Picnics held by ants in ties,
Debating over which pie flies.
As frogs wear hats and sing out loud,
They entertain the curious crowd.

Laughter dances on the breeze,
As nature serves its silliest tease.
A place where joy and giggles freeze,
In this wild world of buzzing ease.

**Fragments of Heaven**

In a patch of grass, a ticklish spot,
The daisies wiggle, like a lot,
While clouds wear socks, oh what a sight!
Bouncing squirrels leap with delight.

A pair of shoes just lost their laces,
Chasing fireflies in funny races.
Giggling worms twist with mirth,
Celebrating their squiggly birth.

Even the sun has a twinkly eye,
Winking at the playful sky.
While rainbows sport their brightest socks,
With colors straight from joke-filled clocks.

Oh, fragments of this heavenly thrill,
Bring laughter with each cozy chill.
In gentle chaos, spirits blend,
In a mosaic of joy without end.

# The Garden Within

Inside my heart, the petals bloom,
With giggles echoing in each room.
A cactus wearing shades of blue,
Sips lemonade from morning dew.

The sunflowers nod as jokes unfold,
With tales of adventures boldly told.
While miniature gnomes take a break,
From baking pies that wobble and shake.

In this inner world, quite absurd,
Where talking stones can be heard.
Every leaf has a punchline bright,
To fill the day and tease the night.

So come and frolic in this zone,
Where every whimsy finds a throne.
In gardens lush, plump with cheer,
Laughter grows anew each year.

## **Sunkissed Serenity**

In a land where sunbeams dance,
The chickens wear shades, take a chance.
Coconuts giggle, swaying high,
As ducks in flip-flops waddle by.

A hammock swings, with a bear's slight snore,
While squirrels make smoothies, what a score!
Flip-flops squeak as tourists roam,
In a place that feels like a joke at home.

## Dappled Mirages

On the beach, a mirage prances,
Where jellyfish wear skirts and take their chances.
Seagulls do yoga in the bright sunlight,
While crabs trade gossip, oh what a sight!

Waves that giggle, tickling toes,
The tide tells secrets a sailor knows.
If you listen closely, you might find,
A fish with a hat, oh, how refined!

**Pride of the Himalayas**

Up in the heights, yaks throw a party,
With ice cream that's cold and a dance that's hearty.
The mountains wear snow like a dazzling dress,
While llamas argue about who's the best!

In the valleys, the yetis rap a tune,
While marmots hold hands under the moon.
A snowman's a judge for a talent show,
Where every creature puts on a glow!

**Through the Mist**

In a world where fog wears a furry hat,
And cats play chess, imagine that!
A slippery eel teaches a class,
While rabbits take notes, oh what a gas!

Winds whisper secrets of popcorn trees,
Where giggling mushrooms dance with ease.
Through the mist, the magic flows,
With whimsy at every turn, who knows?

## Embracing the Current

In a puddle bright, I leap with glee,
Splashing water, oh, look at me!
The fish nearby, they swim with flair,
Winking fins, as if they care.

Rubber ducks with smiles so wide,
They float along on this wild ride.
A swirl, a twirl, a slip, a slide,
Even the turtles can't hide their pride.

Giggling as I soak my shoes,
Wading through laughter, can't lose!
The sunbeam dances, shadows fight,
Who knew mud pies could feel so right?

So come along, let's have some fun,
Create some ripples, on the run!
In every drop, a joke is spun,
Life's a splash, and we have won!

## **Tranquility in Motion**

A driftwood boat, it sways and bobs,
While squirrels toast with tiny cobs.
The breeze whispers secrets, oh so light,
As clouds chase each other, pure delight.

I swear I saw a fish wear shades,
Playing poker with sunlit glades.
The frogs croak songs, like old-time blues,
In this calm realm, no one can lose.

Butterflies float with dainty grace,
Hiccups of laughter in this space.
We twirl and spin in endless glee,
A party where you feel so free!

With every ripple, a smile to share,
Nature's humor fills the air.
So let's embrace the softest way,
And dance with joy throughout the day!

## Shades of Elysium

Under mango trees, I found my throne,
Where laughter rings like crystal tone.
In shades of green and skies so blue,
The world's a candy shop just for you!

A monkey swings with style and flair,
As I sip juice without a care.
Twirling leaves in a playful round,
Each step feels like jumping ground!

The ants march by in a silly line,
With tiny hats, they're feeling fine.
A breeze sprinkles joy, a little fun,
Shadows dance in the warming sun.

So come along, let's join this spree,
In shades of bliss, we're wild and free.
Life's a canvas, let's paint the hue,
With giggles that only we can do!

## **Beauty Beneath the Surface**

In the deep, where secrets swipe,
A clownfish spins, with skills to hype.
The coral giggles in bright array,
As bubbles laugh, then drift away.

A starfish waves from its comfy slot,
With quirky jokes, it hits the spot.
Sea turtles glide without a fuss,
As jellyfish dance, they won't discuss.

The ocean floor, a party grand,
With dancing sands, let's make a stand.
Each wave whispers tales of jest,
Underwater charm, it's simply the best!

So plunge below, don't miss the fun,
Where laughter echoes, never done!
In this wild world of surf and play,
You'll find the joy in every spray!

## Cradle of Tranquility

In a hammock tied to a cow,
I dream of sunny days somehow.
The breeze tickles my nose,
While the grass grows in rows.

Lemonade spills on my toe,
As squirrels put on quite the show.
They dance around, so spry,
As I sip and laugh, oh my!

Bouncing clouds, fluffy and bright,
Play hide and seek, what a sight!
A tune from a bird's beak,
Makes my day feel so unique.

With cool shade from an old tree,
Nature's jokes are wild and free.
Here I giggle and relax,
In my paradise, no cracks.

## Beyond the Veil of Dreams

A hat that can make you fly,
Just watch out for the pie in the sky.
With every leap, I shout,
"Who needs a route?"

Floaty creatures dance around,
They wear shoes that squeak and bound.
We prance on clouds of fluff,
Oh, isn't this fun enough?

A rainbow makes a slippery slide,
With gummy bears as our guide.
We giggle as we race,
In this whimsical space.

When shadows stretch their long arms,
The moon shows off its charms.
We tell jokes to the stars,
And laugh about life's bizarre bars.

## The Breath of Utopia

I inhale the scent of pie,
Blueberry fluff and lemon sky.
Each breath is a sweet feast,
An oddly happy beast.

Dancing shoes on the grass,
Every step is a bright pass.
Chasing rainbows with flair,
Who knew joy could be so rare?

Giggles float through the air,
Like butterflies without a care.
Lollipops grow on trees,
And whisper sweet little tease.

As bubbles rise and pop,
I know the fun won't stop.
In my land of the free,
Joy is the best recipe.

## **Petals in Twilight**

Petals twirl in the breeze,
They dance like cats in trees.
Each color tells a joke,
In twilight's warm yoke.

With butterflies that sing,
And frogs that leap like a king,
The fireflies light the night,
A truly goofy sight.

Twirling 'round with glee,
Laughter spills like tea.
The stars chuckle awake,
As shadows start to break.

In the chaos of bloom,
We find magic in the room.
Here, fun without a worry,
In this delightful flurry.

## **Ripple of Enchantment**

A splash of joy on a sunny day,
Sipped from a cup made of clay.
Fish dance like they know a joke,
While ducks waddle and tease the oak.

Breezes tickle the flowers' faces,
Mischievous ants claim wild races.
Laughter bubbles like soda pop,
In this puddle, fun never stops!

Sunglasses on, we all look cool,
Splashing about, just like in school.
The sun, it winks, and we all grin,
In this magic, where fun begins!

With each wave, silly stories flow,
As we play in nature's show.
A water fight breaks out with glee,
In this realm, we're wild and free!

## **Tranquil Dewdrops**

Morning glistens with tiny beads,
Nature's jewels, fulfilling needs.
Each drop giggles as it rolls down,
On petals bright, like a crown.

Bees buzz by with a humorous flair,
Joking with flowers, a quirky pair.
A ladybug wearing a tiny hat,
Struts down the stem, how about that?

Raindrops tap a silly beat,
Underfoot, slugs shuffle discreet.
Dance of the dew, it brings pure delight,
In the soft glow of morning light!

If a drop could leap and twirl around,
It'd make quite the splash, without a sound.
A dew-dance party, not a dull scene,
In this laughter-filled, shimmering green!

## Essence of the Blossoms

Flower faces grin so bright,
As bees buzz in sheer delight.
Petals shake with laughter grand,
In the garden, where joy's unplanned.

A tulip tries to tell a pun,
But all the daisies just can't run.
Sunlight giggles, kisses the ground,
As earthworms wriggle, spinning round.

Pollen sneezes create a fair,
While butterflies dance without a care.
A rose turns red with giggles loud,
As bees form a jolly, buzzing crowd!

In this bloom-filled, vibrant spree,
Nature's humor is wild and free.
With each chuckle of the dawn,
Life's bouquet of fun is drawn!

## Echoes of the Oasis

In the sand, where camels teeter,
The sun bakes thoughts a little sweeter.
Fluttering fans of palm trees sway,
As lizards laugh at the heat of day.

Mirages giggle, popping up and down,
Tricking the weary who wander around.
Babbling brooks, they tell silly tales,
Of brave little frogs with grandiose scales.

Underneath stars that blink and sway,
Laughter echoes in a playful ballet.
A sip of water feels like a show,
As critters dance in the moonlit glow!

In this haven where fun pervades,
Life's a circus, where joy cascades.
So let's toast to the light and the breeze,
In this oasis, we live with ease!

## Touch of Ambrosia

With every sip, the world does spin,
A taste so sweet, it makes you grin.
Like candy clouds that softly land,
It tickles toes and warms the hand.

Uplifted by this mirthful brew,
I danced a jig, twirled round anew.
My cat joined in, but oh what fell,
He slipped right through like a jellybell!

The neighbors peeped through curtains wide,
To see me bounce, I couldn't hide.
"Is that a party?" they asked loud,
"Just me and joy! Come join the crowd!"

So laughter brewed, the night turned bright,
With giggles shared, we danced till light.
Who knew a sip could bring such cheer?
Next time I'll drink—oh dear, oh dear!

## Enchanted Rain

A shower falls, but not of gloom,
It sparkles light, it makes us zoom.
We skip like frogs through puddles wide,
And laugh at horses that slip and slide.

My umbrella sprouted wings on high,
I chased it down like a bumblefly.
With every splash, we made a scene,
Imitating fish in a goofy green.

The sidewalk turned into our stage,
We took the leap, lost in the age.
Rain coats swirled in our fancy dance,
Each twirl a chance, each fall a glance.

Though drenched and wild, we grinned with might,
For laughter reigned through pure delight.
So prance with me when storm clouds play,
In every drop, we find our way!

## Splashes of Delight

A water fight at noon on fire,
With squirt guns filled, we never tire.
My brother slipped, oh what a sight,
He danced a jig mid-cannons bright.

"Regroup," he yelled, his socks all sogged,
The air was thick, the sunlight bogged.
But dewdrops glistened with each shout,
A dance-off started—who's in doubt?

We laughed like fools, a motley crew,
Performing tricks that no one knew.
The dog joined in with a gleeful bark,
His tail a whip, he hit the mark.

So when the sun begins to blaze,
Gather your pals for splashy plays.
For in each drop of laughter's sound,
True joy is found where fun abounds.

## The Peaceful Torrent

A river flows, but oh what jest,
It whispers tales while we all rest.
With rubber ducks that cruise along,
They quack in tune—a bubbly song.

We toss our woes upon the stream,
And let them float like a funky dream.
I tried to fish, but caught my hat,
It floundered off with a quick little splat!

The sun streamed down, a warming friend,
While splashes flew, would it ever end?
With giggles shared and stories spun,
Each puddle danced in the golden sun.

So if you spy that gentle tide,
Jump in with glee, it's worth the ride.
For in this joyful, watery play,
Every moment's bright—hip, hip hooray!

## **Veils of Enchantment**

In a garden where giggles grow,
Laughter sprinkles down like snow.
Fairies dance in mismatched shoes,
Spreading joy, they share their ruse.

Teacups fly on tiny wings,
With every sip, a songbird sings.
Beware the tickles in the trees,
They'll make you chuckle, if you please.

A hat of flowers, frilly and bright,
Worn by cats who twirl with delight.
They toast the moon, it's quite the sight,
As marshmallow clouds roll in at night.

In this place where pranksters roam,
A puddle sings, "Come, find a home!"
With a wink and a nod, dreams start to tease,
And the world jiggles with glee like cheese.

## Horizons of Delight

Bubbles float like shining dreams,
Tickling toes with playful beams.
On distant shores where giggles leap,
A sandy castle claims its keep.

Seagulls wear sunglasses, strut with flair,
Chasing crabs in a salty dare.
They sing sea shanties, oh so bold,
While the tide tells secrets, old and gold.

Sandcastles wobble, laughter swells,
As jellybeans ring their tiny bells.
Each wave a jest, so free and wild,
Splashing joy, the ocean's child.

With sun-kissed cheeks and salty hair,
We chase our dreams without a care.
The horizon laughs, it twinkles bright,
As we ride waves of pure delight.

## **Sips from the Fountain**

A fountain bubbling, laughter flows,
Spritzing joy with every dose.
Goblins sip in jeweled hats,
Having tea with silly bats.

Each splash a giggle, every drop,
Turns frowns upside-down, makes hearts hop.
With cookies floating, they politely tease,
"Care for a sip? It's sure to please!"

Squirrels wear vests, so grand and fine,
Beneath the fountain, they sip on wine.
While turtles dance, they stomp their feet,
"Drink up, dear friends, make life sweet!"

In this fountain of joyful sprays,
Time tickles by in humorous ways.
So raise your cups, let's celebrate,
For laughter's a potion that's truly great.

## The Allure of Distant Shores

Distant shores call with a wink,
Where fish wear hats and dolphins drink.
They tickle whales with seaweed curls,
As jellyfish twirl in graceful swirls.

A mermaid giggles, bright and spry,
In bubble baths beneath the sky.
She shares tales of treasures found,
While sand dollars dance, all around.

Old pirates boast of silly tricks,
Like riding llamas on roller bricks.
With every wave comes laughter's wave,
In the sea's embrace, we feel so brave.

So, join this frolic, wild and free,
On shores where silliness runs with glee.
Unfurl the sails, let joy take flight,
As we sail away into the night.

## The Fountain of Dreams

In a yard where ducks wear hats,
And trees gossip with their chats,
A fountain spouts a fizzy drink,
I take a sip, and almost wink.

The squirrels dance, all dressed in style,
They drink from cups and laugh awhile,
A turtle's juggling, what a sight!
I'm giggling hard with pure delight.

The fish in suits swim past and joke,
While frogs in bowties learn to poke,
This splashy fun, oh what a scene,
In this small world where joy is keen!

With every splash, a tickle in air,
I throw my worries to despair,
For laughter flows like pearls from spouts,
In my own dreamland, round about.

## Enchanted Waters

There's a pond that shimmers bright,
Where ducks are kings and rule the night,
Fish wear glasses, look so wise,
While frogs perform their acrobatics in the skies.

With every leap, a splash and laugh,
A snail is the judge of every craft,
The water's filled with bubbles rare,
And giggles linger in the air.

A crab in a clown suit takes the stage,
The fish throw popcorn, quite the rage,
While lily pads become the dance floors,
We twirl and spin, shout for encore.

Oh, enchanted waters, how you flow,
With shiny smiles, and life's sweet glow,
In this rib-tickling, joyous place,
I lose myself in the funny space.

**Pure Radiance**

In a bubble bath of sunlit cheer,
A talking turtle draws us near,
He tells us tales of silly dreams,
While golden fish dance in moonbeams.

The water's warm, with giggles near,
Mermaids munch on jelly bears,
From seaweed pools, strange sounds erupt,
As a crab in a bowtie gets all dressed up.

Splashing 'round in pure delight,
A pelican serves snacks, what a sight!
We float in air, as laughter flies,
With sparkling joy and smiling skies.

Pure radiance fills our hearts with cheer,
A world of whimsy, oh so clear,
In this riddle of fun and play,
I plan to stay, oh let me stay!

## Melody of the Rivulet

In a tiny stream of happy tunes,
The fish wear hats made of balloons,
They dance to rhythms, bold and spry,
While dragonflies laugh as they fly by.

A frog with shades croons a song,
The ripples giggle as they flow along,
With every note, the sunbeam smiles,
In this wacky world, happiness piles.

The pebbled shores invite the fun,
To dipsy-doodle, everyone,
A snail breaks out in a funky beat,
As nature groves on shiny feet.

O melody of the rivulet grand,
Where laughter's written in fine sand,
My heart bounces with every trick,
As joys cascade, oh, what a kick!

## Essence of Eden

In the garden where the apples glow,
I tripped on vines and yelled, "Oh no!"
The serpent laughed, oh what a sight,
Said, "Keep your balance—what a flight!"

Bees buzzing round, they wore a crown,
But stung my nose, a joker's frown.
I danced with tulips, slipped on dew,
The flowers winked, "We're laughing too!"

The fruit was sweet but oh, so bold,
I dropped it once, the chaos sold.
The trees all shook with giggles bright,
As I rolled down, such pure delight!

So let us roam in this wild spree,
Where laughter blooms, oh can't you see?
In this Eden, silly and free,
The essence lives in joy, with glee!

## Drifting into Bliss

Floating on clouds of whipped-up cream,
I lost my spoon—what a silly dream!
Marshmallow fluff bounced, oh what fun,
A playful dance in the golden sun.

Ice cream cones adorned with sprinkles bright,
Melted down and took a wild flight.
I chased a scoop, it giggled away,
Like a runaway joke, a soft ballet.

A fizzy river flowed with soda pop,
I slipped and slid—it just wouldn't stop!
Laughter echoed from every wave,
While gummy bears danced, oh so brave.

Joy's in the air, let's take a chance,
In our whimsical, buoyant dance.
Grab a bubble, float and sway,
In this sugary realm, we'll play all day!

## Stories of the River

There once was a stream that told a jest,
With fish that freestyled, they were the best!
A frog in a tuxedo croaked a tune,
While turtles spun tales with a wink and a croon.

The otters, sly, they built a boat,
With candy canes to keep afloat.
They sailed down currents, full of cheer,
While the ducks quacked jokes, so sincere.

Rocks joined in, some silly tunes,
Echoing laughter beneath bright moons.
A splash of whimsy, a flick of the tail,
In the river of giggles, we tell our tale.

So float with the tide, don't hesitate,
For the river's stories are never late.
A splash of joy, a wink and a grin,
In this wild water, let laughter in!

## A Skyward Caress

Clouds shaped like bunnies bounce on high,
While I threw a snowball, oh me, oh my!
The sun's a jester with a golden crown,
Chasing shadows, dancing all around.

Kites soared with squeaks, on strings so tight,
Platforms of giggles in skyward flight.
Birds in tuxedos chirped their glee,
Swooped down low, said, "Join us, you'll see!"

The breeze, a prankster, tickled my nose,
While whispering secrets that only it knows.
A whirlwind of laughter swirled in the air,
Twirled me about without a care.

With each soaring drift, life felt so bright,
In a skyward caress, everything's right.
So let's ride the wind, let ourselves be,
In this joyous flight, oh come and see!

## The Breath of Nature

In a jungle where monkeys prance,
I thought I'd give trees a chance.
They whispered secrets in my ear,
But all I heard was 'Get out of here!'

The breeze tickled my silly nose,
As flowers danced in fancy clothes.
The sun winked from its lofty throne,
I tripped on roots and felt like stone.

Nature's laughter filled the air,
With each rustle, a teasing scare.
I tried to blend with bushes green,
But ended up in grass, unseen!

Yet in this chaos filled with cheer,
I found that silliness is dear.
For laughter blooms where joy ignites,
In nature's realm, as bliss invites.

## Gentle Waters of Splendor

A stream flows by with quirky glee,
It splashes on my open knee.
I giggle as the fish give chase,
Their bubbles pop like laughter's grace.

The frogs hold concerts every night,
With croaks that truly are a sight.
They boost their voices in a row,
While I just sit and steal the show!

The willows sway, their branches bend,
I told them jokes, they did not mend.
With every twist and every sway,
The river seems to sing, 'Hip-hip-hooray!'

How funny how the ripples play,
In nature's humor, lost I stay.
For every splash and every call,
Brings joy that dances, never small.

## **Elysian Flow**

Clouds gather for a water fight,
I take cover, hoping it's light.
They drench me in a laugh-filled spree,
Who knew clouds could be so free?

Raindrops hop like little elves,
Each one trying to show its shelves.
I dance beneath this gleeful rain,
And laugh because I'm not in vain!

The puddles form a mirror's trick,
Reflecting smiles both wide and quick.
I splash around like I belong,
To nature's beat, I just dance along.

And as the sun comes back to shine,
I wave goodbye to rain divine.
With a giggle and a skip in tow,
I chase the clouds, and off we go!

## Lush Cascade

Up on the hill, a waterfall spills,
Where laughter dances with the thrills.
I try to catch drops in my hand,
But they just slip, oh what a stand!

The rocks seem to giggle at my plight,
As I struggle in my silly fight.
But bubbles rise with a cheerful pop,
A nature party I can't stop!

The ferns wave their arms like flags,
While snails parade in tiny bags.
It seems even stones have found a tune,
As I step on one and sing to the moon!

In this cascade of joy so bright,
I learn that laughter is pure delight.
For nature's comedy is best portrayed,
In every drop, where joy won't fade.

## Garden of Nectar

In a patch of flowers, ants dance,
Stealing sweets in a sugar trance.
Bees buzz around, they hum and tease,
While butterflies float like they're on a breeze.

A bumblebee forgot his way,
Stuck in a tulip for the day.
He proclaimed himself the king of sweets,
But he can't even find his feet!

Raining honey, what a splatter,
Squirrels giggle, it's a new matter.
They slip and slide, oh what a mess,
Nature's joy is just pure excess!

The garden laughs with colors bright,
As critters dance beneath the light.
In this paradise of sweet delight,
Every blunder is pure delight!

## A Symphony in Water

A tap that drips a lovely tune,
Echoes softly beneath the moon.
Frogs croak out their nightly song,
With splashes that don't last too long.

A fish flops up to join the jam,
Lands right on a duck, oh what a slam!
The duck quacks loud, "Is this my gig?"
And soon the pond turns into a jig.

Raindrops tap dance on the leaves,
Splashing down to make us believe.
They swirl in circles, laugh about,
While puddles join this joyful shout.

When water's waltzing with the breeze,
We can't help but giggle with ease.
In this wet wonder, fun's the prize,
As laughter sparkles, oh what a surprise!

## Chasing the Sunlight

A little mouse, quite bold and spry,
Wants to catch a sunbeam in the sky.
He jumps and twirls and tumbles down,
    Just chasing light, that silly clown.

Grass tickles his tiny toes,
As his shadow dances, thought it knows.
He trips on clovers, rolls like dough,
    And giggles softly at his show.

Each sunlight chase brings silly falls,
    Attracting ants with tiny calls.
"Catch the light!" they laugh and say,
As shadows mingle in a playful fray.

Oh, what a game of gleeful chase,
With little hearts that race and race.
In this bright play, we all can find,
The sunshine lingers, oh so kind!

## Twilight's Gift

When shadows stretch and evening glows,
Fireflies blink in a line of prose.
The crickets chirp their evening song,
As night unfolds, it won't be long.

A raccoon stumbles in the night,
Searching for snacks, oh what a sight!
He knocks over cans with great delight,
And laughs himself into a fright.

The stars twinkle, sharing winks,
While owls plot hilarious pranks and kinks.
"They can't see us, we're the night's crew!"
And the moon chuckles as if it knew.

In this twilight, laughter spreads,
Among the critters tucked in beds.
With every giggle, the darkness lifts,
As nature shares its nightly gifts!

## Illuminated by Starlight

In the night, the stars they shine,
Like tiny bling on a cosmic line.
I tried to catch one in my hand,
But tripped on my own little stand.

My dog looked up, said, "What's the fuss?"
With a wag and a bark, like, "You're a plus!"
I finally laughed, as I met his gaze,
Who needs the stars? Dogs make my days!

When I lay down for a quiet sleep,
The moon snickers, secrets to keep.
I dreamed of clouds made of cotton candy,
Woke up with drool, how very dandy!

In the morning light, I dared to glance,
At those silly shadows doing a dance.
Can't help but chuckle at nature's tease,
Life's true delights are just a breeze!

## Hues of Elysium

Painting dreams in shades of cheer,
A stroke of laughter, the sun draws near.
Brushes flinging colors of fun,
Like confetti reigns when the day is done.

With every hue, a giggle escapes,
While clouds float by like furry capes.
I named one James, he won't sit still,
Chasing rainbows, what a thrill!

Blues and greens in a playful swirl,
As butterflies spin and twirl.
I wink at the flowers and they blush,
Imagining bees in a friendly hush.

A canvas of smiles, my favorite art,
Each color sings, a joyous heart.
In this whimsical world, I can't confine,
To say it's silly would be just divine!

# The Harmony of Hidden Realms

In gardens where gnomes plot and scheme,
They trade their secrets in a dream.
Each mushroom whispers tales so bright,
Of fairies tossing a raucous fight.

Beneath the leaves, a party brews,
With pizza made of morning dew.
Those pesky squirrels dance on the roof,
Yelling "Free snacks, come get a poof!"

Bamboo flutes make a joyful sound,
As rabbit break dancers spin round.
I once tried to join, but fell on my face,
Now I'm the punchline of this race!

Harmony sings from creatures small,
As they laugh together, inviting us all.
In hidden realms, wonder's the theme,
Living wild laughs, like an endless dream!

## Caress of Sweet Ambrosia

In fields where buttercups gleam like gold,
Got lost in flavors that I'm told.
A sip of nectar, oh what a tease,
Got sticky fingers and a buzzing breeze.

Bees wear tiny hats, looking quite bold,
With dance moves that never get old.
I waved my arms, tried to join in flight,
But fell on my face, what a sight!

Fruit trees giggle, apples in cahoots,
Making pies from their silly fruits.
I burnt my crust, it turned to goo,
The orchard laughed, "We still love you!"

Every taste, a joyful delight,
In this sweet world, I feel so right.
With frolicsome flavors that zings and sways,
Dancing to life in laughter's ways!

## Radiant Dewfall

In the morning's cheeky grin,
Dewdrops dance on blades, akin,
To tiny jewels all around,
They tease the sleepy grass they found.

A ladybug with flair, takes flight,
Wobbling like it's lost the fight,
With every splash that makes them gleam,
It's nature's way of being a meme.

## Trickle of Heaven

Water drips from leaves so sly,
Like a twinkling wink from the sky,
It giggles softly as it spills,
Like hidden secrets, hopeful thrills.

A frog leaps out, all set to cheer,
With leaps that startle, cause a sneer,
It splashes in a pond so blue,
A comedy just for me and you.

## Glimmers of Utopia

The sunbeams tickle every flower,
In this bright, delightful hour,
Petals nodding, what a sight,
In a garden full of pure delight.

A bumblebee in busy sprawl,
Tries to dance, but starts to fall,
Its wobbly twirls make laughter sound,
As it bumbles and goes round and round.

## The Elixir of Dawn

Morning brews a cup of charm,
A potion that shall do no harm,
With laughter brewing in the steam,
It tickles senses with a dream.

Sipping sunlight, what a treat,
With giggles sweet and hearty beat,
The day begins with joyous flair,
As nature's comedy fills the air.

## A Journey Through Ethereal Fields

In fields where giggles grow so tall,
The butterflies wear pants, not small.
They dance around the clumsy bees,
In shoes of grass, they trip with ease.

The clouds are made of cotton candy,
In this place, the skies feel dandy.
The daisies talk and tell silly jokes,
As the lollipops join in with pokes.

Silly rabbits hop with flair,
And sing duet with the fragrant air.
While rainbows leave their paint to dry,
As carrots skate and onions fly.

Each step we take brings laughter clear,
In this land, we lose all fear.
Frolics here are never done,
We chase the joy, we chase the fun.

## Seasons of Joy

When springtime giggles start to bloom,
And flowers bounce around the room.
The raindrops fall like silly hats,
As puddles call to playful cats.

Summer brings a sunburned cheer,
With ice cream trucks that disappear.
The sunflowers wear shades on high,
While bumblebees practice their fly.

Fall leaves rustle with a tease,
As pumpkins roll down with the breeze.
The squirrels dance in furry frights,
While acorns have their thumping fights.

Winter wraps us all in snow,
With snowmen joining in the show.
They twirl and laugh, they toss a snow
And ski down hills with a squeaky "whoa!"

## The Taste of Enchanted Days

On mornings filled with cereal rain,
The spoons become a joyful train.
With milk rivers and fruit trees bright,
Breakfast parties take to flight.

Lunch rolls out with sandwiches fun,
As crusts become a playful gun.
With chips that sing and soda that dances,
Every bite leads to wild prances.

Dinner comes with pizza pies,
As broccoli wears big, green ties.
The forks all giggle, knives take a bow,
As laughter fills the room, oh wow!

Desserts arrive with cakes adorned,
Whipped cream parties, sweetly scorned.
Chocolate rivers flowing wide,
In blissful bites, we take the ride.

## Dance of the Luminous Sky

The stars are dressed in shiny gowns,
As planets spin and lose their frowns.
In cosmic balls, they swirl and sway,
While comets throw confetti play.

The moon, a jester, winks and grins,
As laughter echoes 'round the spins.
The meteors join in a quick chase,
With cosmic dust tucked in their space.

A waltz of galaxies unfolds,
In hues of purple, blue, and golds.
The suns all giggle, brighter still,
As time drifts by, it's quite the thrill.

In this ballet of cosmic cheer,
Each twinkle shouts, "Come dance right here!"
With gravity just a gentle whim,
We're lost in joy, we laugh and swim.

## Essence of Bliss

In the fridge, a jar of glee,
Pickle juice that calls to me.
Salsa dancing with the cheese,
Life's a laugh, if you just seize.

Mustard plays the trumpet loud,
While ketchup stands, so very proud.
They squirt confetti on the fries,
In this banquet of surprise!

Soda bubbles, giggles burst,
In the chaos, quench your thirst.
Join the feast, don't miss the fun—
Gourmet jokes for everyone!

Desserts jump like a springing skip,
With every bite, they make you flip.
Cake's a joker with its layers,
In this kitchen, we're the players.

## **Nectar of the Morning**

Bees buzz in with coffee dreams,
Splashing cream with silly themes.
Toast is juggling, jam's the clown,
Croissants dance, but don't fall down.

Eggs are winking on the plate,
Bacon's laughing, isn't fate great?
A pancake stacks like towers tall,
Syrup diving—what a fall!

Cereal does the morning jig,
As spoons and bowls play tag, so big.
Oatmeal hums a sleepy tune,
While yogurt swims with a little spoon.

Muffins tumble, making mess,
"Eat me first!" they shout, no stress.
With morning humor, start your quest,
In this breakfast, we are blessed.

## Celestial Drizzle

Raindrops giggle on the ground,
Each one's got a joke profound.
Puddles splash like kids at play,
In this shower, come what may!

Umbrellas sway, a dance so fine,
Splish-splash laughter, feeling divine.
Clouds wear hats, fluffy and round,
While raincoats twirl, joy unbound.

Sunshine peeks with a wink and grin,
Chasing raindrops like a kin.
Rainbows giggle, colors bright,
Painting smiles, what pure delight!

Nature giggles in this spree,
With a drizzle, just let it be.
Splashing fun, under the sky,
Join this dance; come let's fly!

## Heart of the Garden

Veggies chatting, roots take a stand,
In the dirt, they form a band.
Carrots groove, with leafy flair,
Tomatoes blush, they love the air.

Zucchini plays a daring game,
While peppers yell, "We're not so tame!"
Insects buzzing with delight,
Bees and blooms share merry sight.

Digging deep, the earth's a laugh,
Worms can't help but dance and chaff.
Sunflowers guard the merry lot,
In this spot, we hit the jackpot.

Harvest time, let's toast and cheer,
With fruits and veggies all so dear.
Laughter sprouted, joy's a friend,
In the garden, fun won't end!

## **Reflections of Bliss**

In a puddle, I found my fate,
My hair's a mess, oh isn't it great?
A dog jumped in, splashed with glee,
Now I'm wet, but that's just me!

Mirrors of water, so much to see,
My face is funny, like a big bumblebee.
I wink at the clouds, they giggle back,
We share this moment, you see it's a whack!

Dancing shadows on the ground,
Each funny face, a joy unbound.
Silly squirrels join in the play,
In the puddles, we laugh all day!

So jump right in, leave worries behind,
Life's little puddles can be quite kind.
With a splash and a grin, we move with delight,
Finding bliss in our own silly sight.

## Echoes of Celestial Light

Stars fell down, what an odd sight,
One landed here, oh what a fright!
It tripped on a cat, made the dog bark,
Had us all rolling, laughing till dark!

I called up the moon, said 'Hey, join us!'
He chuckled with glee, what a fuss!
With each twinkle, a joke he'd share,
Like cosmic stand-up, floating in the air.

Planets are whirling, gravity's wobbly,
Each step we take, we're all kind of bobbly.
Galactic giggles, we can't get enough,
In this universe, we're always up to stuff!

So spin with the stars, let the laughter ignite,
In this celestial circus, everything feels right.
With echoes of light, the night's full of cheer,
Each funny little moment draws us all near!

**The Secret in the Dew**

Morning dew drops, so fresh and bright,
I found a fairy, she took flight!
With a sprinkle of laughter, she danced around,
Telling secrets in whispers, oh, what a sound!

She said, 'Watch out, the grass may tickle!'
By then, I fell, and it made me giggle!
Eavesdropping ants, with tiny ears,
Joined our laughter, dispelled my fears.

The sun peeked through, glistening rays,
Made the droplets dance in playful plays.
They shimmered and shone, a tiny parade,
While I just giggled, and felt unafraid.

So chase the dew, catch that whim,
In every droplet, life's never dim.
With laughter and cheer, we glide and sway,
Living in secrets, come join the play!

## Chasing Hopes in the Ether

Floating dreams on cotton candy clouds,
Whispers of jokes from the laughing crowds.
I reached for a hope, but it slipped away,
Landed in a pie; oh, what a display!

With each twinkle of light, a new chance,
Every giggle echoing, making me dance.
The ether's alive with chuckles and fun,
I'm chasing these hopes till the day is done!

Balloons of laughter drift through the air,
Chasing each hope without a care.
If life's a circus, I'm front row seat,
With clowns and confetti, it's all quite a treat!

So run after dreams, like bubbles they rise,
With each silly moment, we touch the skies.
In the laughter we find, the hopes that we tether,
Together we float, light as a feather!

www.ingramcontent.com/pod-product-compliance
Lightning Source LLC
Chambersburg PA
CBHW072215070526
44585CB00015B/1351